LITO

The Shoeshine Boy

LITO

The Shoeshine Boy

as told to and translated by

David Mangurian

photographs by David Mangurian

by Lito Chirinos

Four Winds Press New York

Library of Congress Cataloging in Publication Data

Lito The Shoeshine boy
    SUMMARY: An eleven-year-old shoeshine boy in Honduras tells about his daily life.
      1. Children, Vagrant – Tegucigalpa – Personal narratives – Juvenile literature.   2. Chirinos, Lito.
[1. Honduras – Social conditions.   2. Children in Honduras] I. Mangurian, David.   II. Title.
HV747.H6C5   301.44'1   74-26826
ISBN 0-590-07382-6

Published by Four Winds Press
A Division of Scholastic Magazines, Inc., New York, N.Y.
Copyright © 1975 by David Mangurian

Library of Congress Catalog Card Number: 74-26826
1   2   3   4   5   79   78   77   76   75

To kids everywhere

Every city in the world has its homeless children – unwanted children abandoned by their parents. Their homes are the streets. Sometimes they travel together in packs. More often they wander by themselves, because each one is competing against the other for whatever the city will give him each day.

They sell newspapers, candy, gum, shine shoes. They carry packages for women in the markets or luggage for people at bus and train stations. They guard parked cars at night. Sometimes they steal. They survive entirely by themselves. Survival is their only goal.

Lito Chirinos is one of them. He shines shoes and sells newspapers. I was photographing for UNICEF in Tegucigalpa, the hot dry capital of Honduras, Central America. I was just finishing lunch in a cheap restaurant when Lito came in, shoeshine box hung over his shoulder. He asked for the leftovers on my plate. He said his mother was from a country town and had left him here three years before. He had supported himself ever since.

We became quick friends. For four days I followed him with my cameras down miles of Tegucigalpa's gray-tiled sidewalks, through the markets, and into the cheap restaurants, coffee shops, *cantinas,* and billiard halls that are Lito's life.

This is what I observed and wrote down about him then:

Lito's worldly possessions:

1. One pair of pants with worn-out seat.
2. One short-sleeved shirt.
3. One gray, sleeveless sweater.
4. One shiny automobile wheel lug.
5. An old black cord from an electric iron.

6. A small round plastic tin for Vaseline to plaster down his curly hair.

7. A red wooden shoeshine box stuffed with cans of polish, a bottle for water, and some rags.

He spent most of his waking hours working — shining shoes and selling newspapers on certain days of the week. He was good at it. But few people care who shines their shoes or sells them a paper. So his earnings were directly proportional to the number of people (potential customers) he came in contact with each day. He averaged the equivalent of $1.00 a day — more than most other kids make. To do it he worked twelve to fourteen hours and walked about ten miles every day.

Lito had a huge appetite. He was only twelve or thirteen years old (he didn't know for sure). But when we stopped to eat, he ate more than I did. And even though I was buying his food, he continued to spend most of what he earned on snacks during the day. He said he had worms in his stomach.

Once I asked him: "When you beg, don't you mind eating leftover food from somebody else's plate?"

He smiled. "No," he said, "We're all Hondurans."

Like all poor people, Lito had the ability to hide the worst side of his own life from himself. I think it helped him to go on living, to survive. Lito never got ahead of the game. Each morning the struggle to get enough food began all over again. But he never gave up. The will to survive is too strong.

I can't tell you any more because I've never even gone twenty-four hours without eating. But Lito can. These are his words.

My name is Lito. Lito Chirinos.

I was born in a small town in the province of Olancho. I didn't
know my father very well. When my mother began living with

my father, they built a brick house. But my mother fought with
my father. Then my mother got sick and she went to the city to

get cured. When she returned my father had already sold the brick house and everything. So we left with my mother for another town.

I was about five or six when I began shining shoes. My brother was a shoeshine boy. He loaned me an extra shoeshine box and I started going around. I was very young, and it was the only work I could do. When I wasn't shining shoes I used to go with my mother to the fields to pick black beans.

When I was, let's see, about nine years old, we came to the city. We were walking in the market when my mother said to me: "Do you want to stay here?"

"No," I told her. Then she hit me. She hit me a lot, and then she walked off and left me there.

A woman in the market gave me a place to sleep. She sells corn *tortillas*. She gives me a place to sleep and I give her my money.

Seven of us sleep there: me, another kid my age who shines shoes, a younger kid, a baby who can't walk, a girl seven, the *Señora,* and her son who's nineteen and works as a bricklayer.

It's a little room. There's a door and a window. And a small stove. That's all. The middle is dirt. It doesn't have any water. Not even a tap. We get water from a faucet about four or five blocks from here.

The beds are made of wood and are strung with hemp cord. Across that is cardboard and some pieces of straw mats, and across that a torn blanket. And there are fleas. Little bugs that bite you. They crawl around on the floor.

The house is just a little room and it doesn't have a yard.

The neighborhood where I live is called "The Little Crosses."
It's by the cemetery. At night it's dangerous. There are lots of
thieves. One time we were coming back from a circus. You know
what a circus is? We were coming back, and there was a man all
stabbed and his mother was crying. And now people are afraid
to pass there at midnight.

Me, I'm scared to pass the cemetery at night. I'm scared the
ghosts might jump out and grab me and make me *loco*. Tear me
apart. So I look for another shoeshine boy at night and go back
to the house with him.

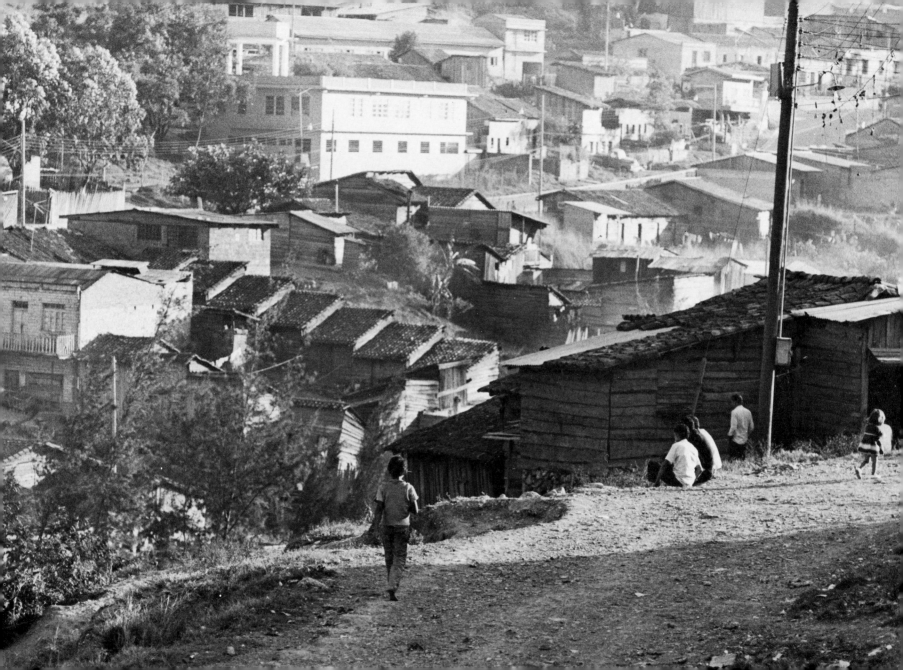

I go to the city early to shine shoes.

I walk all over the city. There are so

    many shoeshine boys.

I look for places where they don't go.

I have to walk a lot.

People give me fifteen or twenty *centavos* for a shine. Sometimes they give me ten. There are some people who give me fifty *centavos*.

And there are some people who want to give me just five.

Yeah, and sometimes I spend all my money
on things to eat. I eat it up in candy, oranges,
bananas, rolls, everything. I could drink Pepsi
Cola all day long. And ice cream, it's delicious!

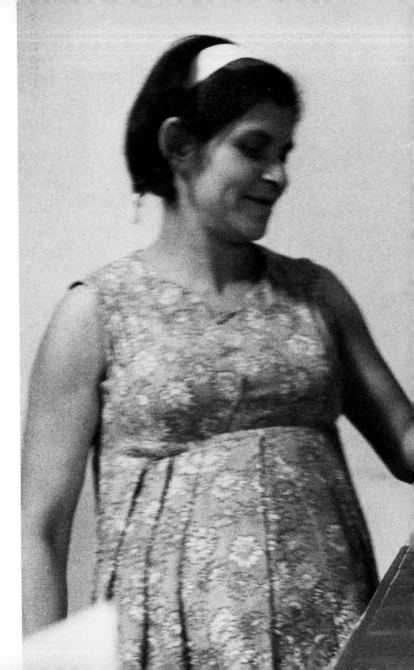

And what I have left at night I take to the *Señora*. When I only do a few shines, I take her only thirty *centavos,* or twenty. On those days, sometimes she hits me.

In Olancho I was in the first grade. But when my mother brought me here, I didn't continue in school. You can only go to school if another person registers you. You have to be signed in and paid for. But the *Señora* doesn't want to sign me in.

Some days I sell newspapers.
I go around selling with my
shoeshine box over my shoulder.
I go everywhere.

There are restaurants where it's prohibited.
But I sneak inside. Sometimes the waitress
grabs me by the ear and runs me out.

And sometimes I swear back at her and snap
this cord I carry at her and then I run.

I beg food in the saloons and restaurants. Chicken, chop suey, chops, fish – lots of things. Anything they'll give me – *tortillas,* bread, spaghetti, rice, coffee, tea – anything. Sometimes it's good, sometimes bad. Sometimes people buy me food and give it to me.

Dinner I buy. I get black beans, cheese, corn *tortillas,* and coffee. Sometimes it costs me up to seventy-five *centavos* because I have such a big appetite.

But there are some days when I don't eat. Because there are some days when I don't do any shines. People don't get their shoes shined when it's raining. The day is ruined.

So I walk around, see, with my mouth open catching flies because there's nothing to eat. I feel empty. I get a bad pain in my belly like something hot down there.

And when I don't eat, the worms do like this

brrrrrrrrrrrrrrrrrr

like a motor, asking for food. The worms I have. And when they're full, my guts go

chee-chee-chee-chee

in my belly. It's bad.

pahzz.....PAHZZ!

Listen

brrrrrrrrrrrrrrrrrr

See how my guts are going now. The worms are hungry. They haven't eaten since morning.

I have two true friends.

Virgilio and Hector.

We call Virgilio "Churro" and Hector "Django."

On me they stuck the name "The Naked Donkey." They saw me once when I was washing my clothes on a big rock on the bank of the river.

Churro's my best friend.

→ 4A   → 5   → 5A   → 6   → 6A   → 7   → 7A   → 8
                                                                              KODAK TRI X PAN FILM

→ 12A   → 13   → 13A   → 14   → 14A   → 15   → 15A   → 16

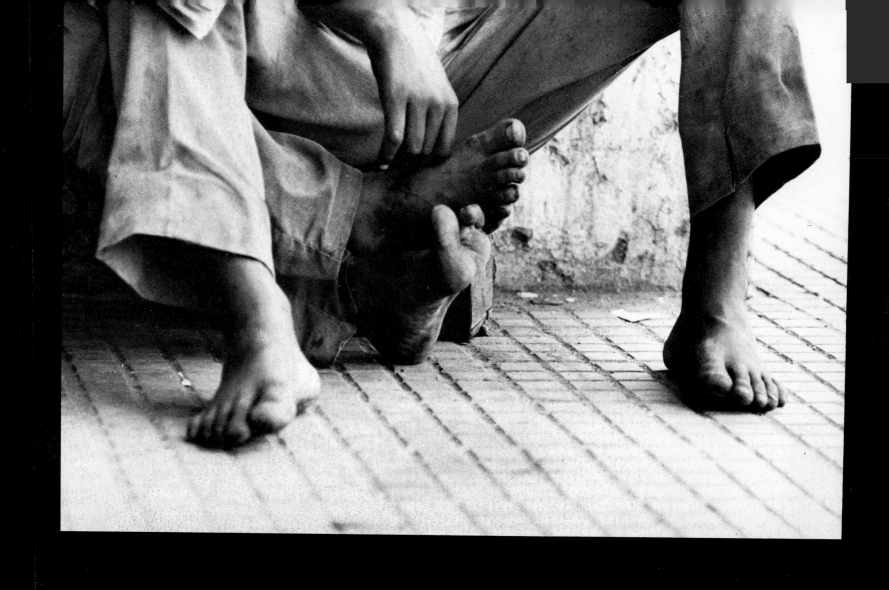

Churro says that his mother didn't want him or his sister either. His sister's young. She lives with an old guy in Olancho. She was always hitting Churro. So he came here to the city by himself. He just wanders around. A woman gives him a place to sleep. He gets food at a place where a friend of ours lives.

That's why the life we have is the saddest life in the world. Like we were orphans.

Well, that's my life. Just working. I work every day, every week, every month. I have my birthday like I'm not having a birthday. I don't have any new clothes to show off or anything. I don't even know what day it is. I work. And on Christmas I work harder.

I don't like to rest. I don't like doing nothing. Maybe going around playing one day or going to a swimming pool or to a beach. But I don't like being alone in the house. I think of sad things, ugly things. Like killing. It makes me want to cry. That's why you won't find me resting.

I walk so much that by the end of the day I can't walk any more. I get lumps in my legs from walking so much. The only way they go away is if I lie down. When I go home, I go straight to bed.

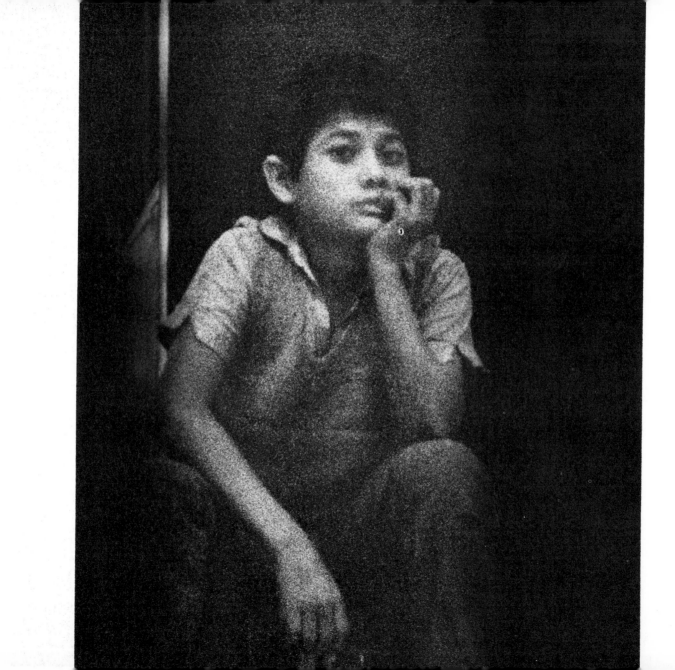

When I'm a man, when I'm nineteen, I want to learn a trade. Like shoemaker, bricklayer, carpenter, bus driver, chauffeur, whatever. I want to buy everything I need – clothes, shoes, a radio, a bed, a house. A brick house. And help my mother.

And marry. But not until I'm a man. I'm still young. I want to have a lot of children. I'll stick them in school so they learn to read and write. Because if you don't know how to read and write, you stay dumb.

Me, I'm dumber than the lizards. The poor guy is dumb and the rich guy is clever. Poor people just smell the food cooking while rich people stuff themselves. You're rich! Yeah! You eat three times a day.

But someday my life will change. Someday I'll get lucky.

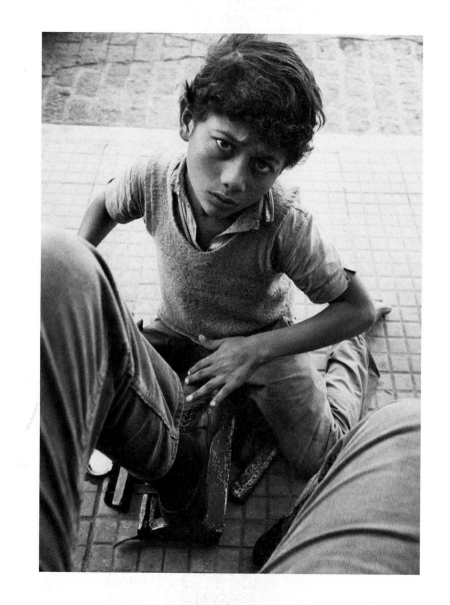

The day I left Tegucigalpa I bought Lito a jacket, pants, and shoes. He looked proud all dressed up, but I always suspected it must have hurt his business badly for a while. He looked so prosperous.

A year and a half later I returned to Honduras on another assignment. After searching two days I found Lito and Churro.

They hadn't changed much. Churro had grown taller and was beginning to look like a young man. But Lito was still a boy and just as cocky as before. He was still wearing the pants I bought for him, but he was barefoot. I don't think he ever got used to the shoes.

I took them to eat. Lito still had his old appetite.

"Lito, would you really like to learn a trade, something you can do besides shining shoes?" I asked.

"Yeah, sure," he said.

I took Lito and Churro to the outskirts of Tegucigalpa where Sister María Rosa had built her "Children's City" for abandoned kids like them. I had done a magazine story on the project, and everyone there knew me. They had just started a workshop to teach shoemaking and carpentry to their older children after school.

The director, Father Guillermo, said they often had problems taking children Lito's age who had grown used to the independence of street life. Young children adapted more easily, he said.

"But he's a bright boy," I said. "The streets haven't turned him bad yet. If he doesn't at least learn how to read and write, he has no future at all."

"I know," said the priest. "But there are so many other children, and we're already crowded. The little ones work out better."

"Will you take him as a favor to me," I said. "I can give you $100 toward his costs."

"All right," he said finally. "But don't be disappointed if he doesn't stay long."

He showed Lito around. Then I told him it was his decision whether to stay or not.

"Can Churro stay too?" he asked.

"Impossible," the priest said to me. "He's even older than Lito."

I told Lito. "Can Churro come out and see me?" he asked.

The priest said he could, the first Sunday every month. More frequent visits tended to draw children back to the streets.

Lito wanted to think about it overnight. I took him and Churro back to the city and left them. Early the next morning Lito showed up alone at my hotel. His hair was slicked down with a little Vaseline. He was quiet and nervous.

"I'll try it," he said.

We took a taxi out. They took his name and asked him a lot of questions and put the information down on their forms. I was just as nervous as Lito. Then they called a man who came with a VW bus. "He'll take you to your new home," they said.

We embraced. Lito got into the bus and pressed his face against the window. Tears were streaming down his cheeks. They were running down mine too as he drove off.

I left Honduras that same day for South America. I wrote Lito every so often. Of course, he couldn't write back. He didn't know how to write.

Several months later one of my letters came back unopened. It took me a moment to realize what happened. The priest had been right. Apparently Lito had not adapted to the regular meals, regular showers, regular hours, and regular classes at the children's home and finally ran away to join his friend Churro on the streets of Tegucigalpa again. Or perhaps he went back to Olancho to look for his mother, hoping she'd finally take him back.

I still have the unopened letter. I don't know why I keep it. I have no other address for him. People sometimes ask me how they can help Lito. I don't have any answer for them.